The Children's Song Book

Edited and introduced by
Michael Foss

Music arranged by
John White

Illustrated by
Gail Lewton

First Published in The United States of America 1979 by
Chartwell Books Inc
A division of Book Sales Inc
110 Enterprise Avenue
Secaucus, New Jersey 07094

©The Rainbird Publishing Group Limited 1979

This Book was designed and produced by
The Rainbird Publishing Group Limited
36 Park Street
London W1Y 4DE

House editor: Beverley Moody
Designer: Pauline Harrison

Library of Congress Catalog Number 79-55451
ISBN 0-89009-310-5

All rights reserved. No part of this
publication may be reproduced, stored in a
retrieval system or transmitted in any form
or by any means, electronic, mechanical, recording
or otherwise, without the prior
permission of the Publisher.

Text filmset by W.S. Cowell Ltd, Ipswich, Suffolk, England
Music filmset by Caligraving Limited, Thetford, Norfolk, England
Printed and bound in Hong Kong by
South China Printing Co. Limited

Contents

Introduction 7

Nursery Songs
Hey Diddle Diddle, the Cat and the Fiddle 10
Little Bo-Peep 12
Ladybird, Ladybird, Fly Away Home 14
Jack and Jill 16
The Little Nut Tree 17
The Mocking Bird 18
Baa Baa Black Sheep 20
Georgy Porgy 22
Three Blind Mice 24

Dancing Songs
Oranges and Lemons 28
London Bridge is Broken Down 30
A Ring o' Roses 32
You Turn for Sugar 34
Here We Go Round the Mulberry Bush 36
We're Marching Round the Levee 37
Sally Go Round the Sunshine 38

American Songs
Mister Frog 42
Short'nin' Bread 44
The Blue-Tail Fly 46
Shanghai Chicken 48
Bullfrog 50
The Train is A-Coming 52
The Story of Creation 54
The Old Grey Goose 56
Colorado Trail 57
What's Little Babies Made Of? 58
Mister Rabbit 60
Little Bird, Go Through My Window 62
A Little Boy Threw His Ball 64
The Mermaid 66
Old Ponto is Dead 68
The American Stranger 70
Captain Kidd 72

Traditional English Songs

The Hunt is Up 76
The Maid and the Miller 77
The Old Woman Tossed 78
The Fox and the Grapes 80
There Was a Monkey Climbed Up a Tree 82
The Sluggard 84
Three Jovial Welshmen 86
Spanish Ladies 88
Doctor Faustus 89
Tom the Piper's Son 90
The Fox and the Goose 92
How Doth the Little Busy Bee 94
Sing Ivy 96
My Boy Willie 98
Scarborough Fair 100
Adieu to Old England 102
Three Maidens A-Milking Did Go 104
Yankee Doodle 106
The Holly and the Ivy 108
As I Sat on a Sunny Bank 109
The Bitter Withy 110

Songs of Scotland and Ireland

O Dear What Can the Matter Be? 114
Up in the Morning Early 116
Auld King Cole 118
Rattling, Roaring Willie 120
If I Was a Blackbird 121
The Kerry Recruit 122
The Magpie's Nest 124
I Know Where I'm Going 125
Down by the Salley Gardens 126

Index 128

Introduction

Old words and old music, said Cecil Sharp, that great collector who rescued so many traditional songs, make a small demand, merely wanting 'to be known, and to be loved.' To claim too much for the songs brought together in this book would be wrong: it is enough to say that each one has given private joy to generations of children wherever English – in all its shades and dialects – is spoken.

A modern habit foolishly makes a great divide between the things of childhood and those of the adult. Many of these songs are specifically *for* children – lullabies, game-songs, nonsense songs, nursery rhymes, etc. But a growing child must see and understand the adult world, and to sing the traditional songs of life and work that arise in unsophisticated communities is a very good preparation for maturity. Working men and women lighten their daytime burden with songs, and at night, for entertainment and delight, sing again the old matter of their traditions. Children love these songs too, and through the modest ritual of learning them from the adults, are incorporated into the community.

For all these songs belong, in some sense, to folk tradition. And so long as they are repeated they are still living and still changing: each generation, perhaps even each singer, makes alterations in both words and music. We have gone back as far as we can, compared as many versions as possible, and chosen the versions which seem freshest and most vital. This kind of folk song, as the editors of *The Oxford Book of Carols* have written, 'may have faults of grammar, logic and prosody,' but it has the charm of innocent view and simple language wedded to a melody that stays in the mind. Whatever the faults of construction, the songs that live – those collected here – do so because of their sincerity.

Michael Foss

These songs come from a great variety of backgrounds, and though originally sung unaccompanied, seemed to suggest, in their particular ways, specific instrumental accompaniments, such as bagpipes, mouth-organ, banjo, harmonium or whatever. Intuitions as to these kinds of accompaniment helped me in the choice of pianistic layout which will, I hope, discreetly add local colour and character to the charm and vigour of these timeless melodies.

John White

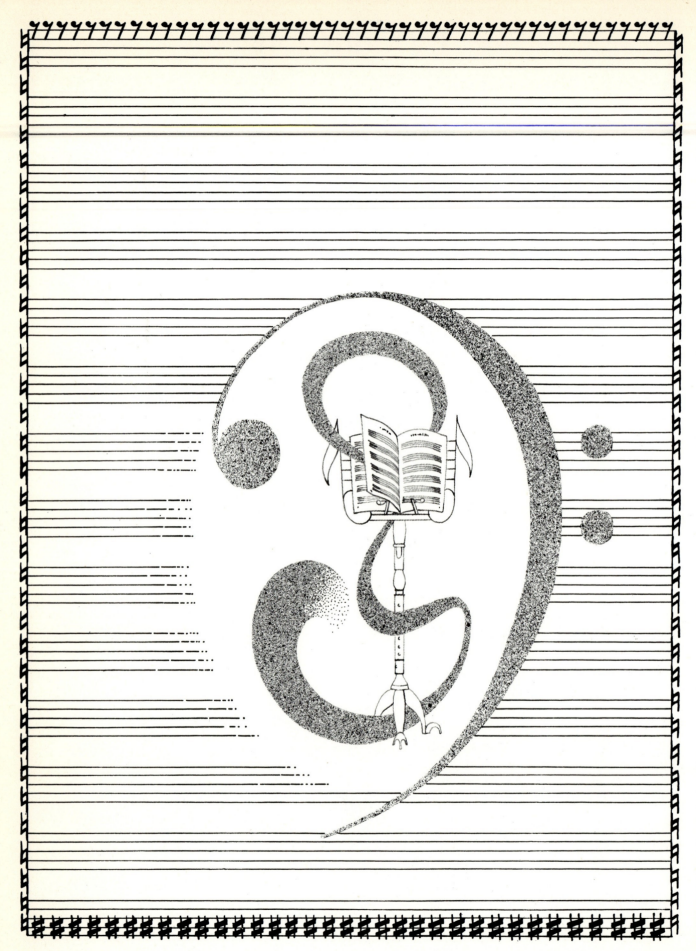

Hey Diddle Diddle, the Cat and the Fiddle

Hey diddle diddle, the cat and the fiddle,
The cow jumped over the moon;
The little dog laughed to see such fun,
And the dish ran away with the spoon.

3 Then she took her little crook,
   Determined for to find them;
   She found them indeed, but it made her heart bleed,
   For they'd left their tails behind them.

4 She heaved a sigh and wiped her eye,
   And o'er the hills went rambling,
   And tried what she could, as a shepherdess should,
   To tack a tail to its lambkin.

Ladybird, Ladybird, Fly Away Home

(Steady ♩. Music for v.3 runs from 𝄋 to end, melody written with stems down)

La-dy-bird, la-dy-bird, Fly a-way home, Your house is on fire And your child-ren are gone.

Fly a-way La-dy-bird, Fly a-way home, Your house is on fire And your child-ren are gone.

1 Ladybird, ladybird,
  Fly away home,
  Your house is on fire
  And your children are gone.

2 Fly away ladybird,
  Fly away home,
  Your house is on fire
  And your children are gone.

3 All except one,
  And that's little Ann,
  And she has crept under
  The frying-pan.

Jack and Jill

1 Jack and Jill went up the hill
   To fetch a pail of water.
   Jack fell down and broke his crown,
   And Jill came tumbling after.

2 Up Jack got, and home did trot,
   As fast as he could caper.
   He went to bed to mend his head,
   With vinegar and brown paper.

The Little Nut Tree

1 I had a little nut tree,
   Nothing would it bear
   But a silver nutmeg
   And a golden pear.

2 The King of Spain's daughter
   Came to visit me,
   And all for the sake
   Of my little nut tree.

3 I skipped o'er the ocean,
   I danced o'er the sea,
   And all the birds in the air
   Couldn't catch me.

The Mocking Bird

(Swinging ♩. Bracketed rhythms account for variations in *vs.* 2–8.)

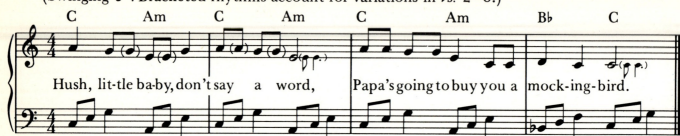

Hush, lit-tle ba-by, don't say a word, Papa's going to buy you a mock-ing-bird.

1 Hush, little baby, don't say a word,
  Papa's going to buy you a mocking-bird.

2 If that mocking-bird don't sing,
  Papa's going to buy you a diamond ring.

3 If that diamond ring turns to brass,
  Papa's going to buy you a looking-glass.

4 If that looking-glass gets broke,
  Papa's going to buy you a Billy-goat.

5 If that Billy-goat won't pull,
  Papa's going to buy you a cart and bull.

6 If that cart and bull turn over,
  Papa's going to buy you a dog named Rover.

7 If that dog named Rover won't bark,
  Papa's going to buy you a horse and cart.

8 If that horse and cart fall down,
  You'll be the sweetest girl in town.

Baa Baa Black Sheep

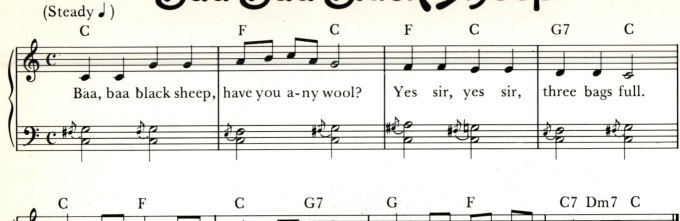

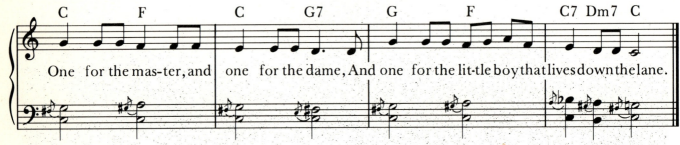

Baa, baa, black sheep, have you any wool?
Yes sir, yes sir, three bags full.
One for the master, and one for the dame,
And one for the little boy that lives down the lane.

Three blind mice, see how they run!
They all ran after the farmer's wife,
Who cut off their tails with a carving knife,
Did you ever see such a thing in your life,
As three blind mice.

Oranges and Lemons

Oranges and lemons,
Say the bells of St Clement's.

You owe me five farthings,
Say the bells of St Martin's.

When will you pay me?
Say the bells of Old Bailey.

When I grow rich,
Say the bells of Shoreditch.

When will that be?
Say the bells of Stepney.

I do not know,
Says the great bell of Bow.

Here comes a candle to light you to bed,
And here comes a chopper to chop off your head.

London Bridge is Broken Down

(Fast ♩.)

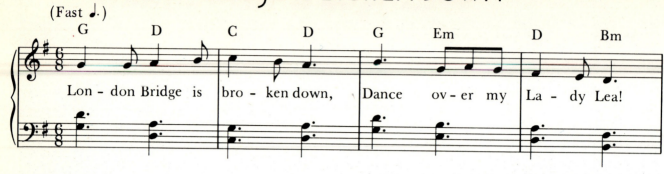

1. London Bridge is broken down,
   Dance over my Lady Lea!
   London Bridge is broken down,
   My fair lady.

2. Build it up with wood and clay,
   Dance over my Lady Lea!
                   Etc.

3. Wood and clay will wash away,
   Dance over my Lady Lea!
                   Etc.

4 Build it up with iron and steel,
   Dance over my Lady Lea!
                              Etc.

5 Iron and steel will bend and bow,
   Dance over my Lady Lea!
                              Etc.

6 Build it up with silver and gold,
   Dance over my Lady Lea!
                              Etc.

7 Silver and gold will be stolen away,
   Dance over my Lady Lea!
                              Etc.

8 Build it up with stone so strong,
   Dance over my Lady Lea!
   That will last for ages long,
   My fair lady.

A Ring o' Roses

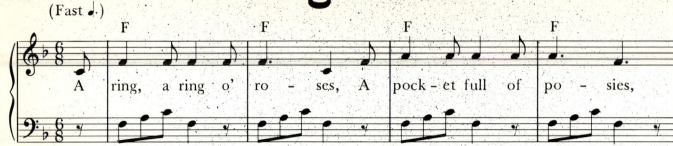

1. A ring, a ring o' roses,
   A pocket full of posies,
   Ash-a, ash-a,
   All fall down.

2. The king has sent his daughter
   To fetch a pail of water,
   Ash-a, ash-a,
   All fall down.

3. The parson in the steeple
   Is preaching to the people,
   Ash-a, ash-a,
   All fall down.

4. The wedding bells are ringing,
   The boys and girls are singing,
   Ash-a, ash-a,
   All fall down.

You Turn for Sugar

1 You turn for sugar an' tea,
I turn for candy,
Boys all love that sugar an' tea,
Girls all love that candy.
You turn, I turn,
You turn, I turn.

2 Some ladies love that sugar an' tea,
Some ladies love candy,
Some ladies wheel all around
An' kiss their loves so handy.
Chorus

3 Miss Brown sure loves sugar an' tea,
Miss Brown sure loves candy,
Miss Brown sure can turn all around
And kiss her true love handy.
Chorus

Here We Go Round the Mulberry Bush

(Fast ♩.)

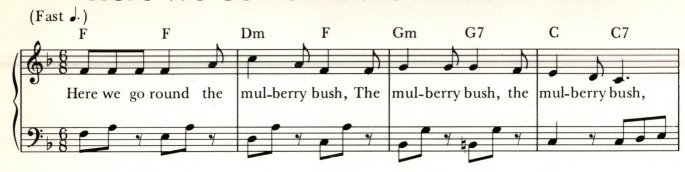

1 Here we go round the mulberry bush,
   The mulberry bush, the mulberry bush,
   Here we go round the mulberry bush,
   On a cold and frosty morning.

2 This is the way we wash our hands,
   Wash our hands, wash our hands,
                              Etc.

3 This is the way we brush our hair,
   Brush our hair, brush our hair,
                              Etc.

4 This is the way we brush our clothes,
   Brush our clothes, brush our clothes,
                              Etc.

5 This is the way we go to school,
   Go to school, go to school,
                              Etc.

We're Marching Round the Levee

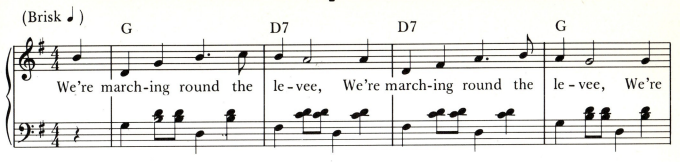
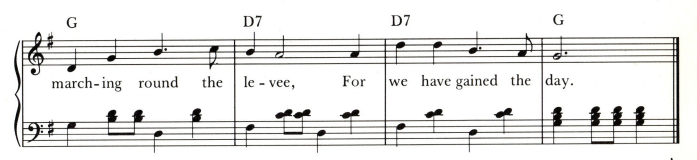

1 We're marching round the levee,
We're marching round the levee,
We're marching round the levee,
For we have gained the day.

2 Go forth and face your lover,
　　　　　　　　　　etc.
For we have gained the day.

3 I kneel because I love you,
　　　　　　　　　　etc.
For we have gained the day.

4 Good-bye I hate to leave you,
　　　　　　　　　　etc.
For we have gained the day.

5 I'm coming back to see you,
　　　　　　　　　　etc.
For we have gained the day.

Sally Go Round the Sunshine

(Fast ♩)

Sally go round the sun
Sally go round the moon
Sally go round the sunshine
Every afternoon Boom! Boom!

Sally go round the sun,
Sally go round the moon,
Sally go round the sunshine,
Every afternoon,
Boom! Boom!

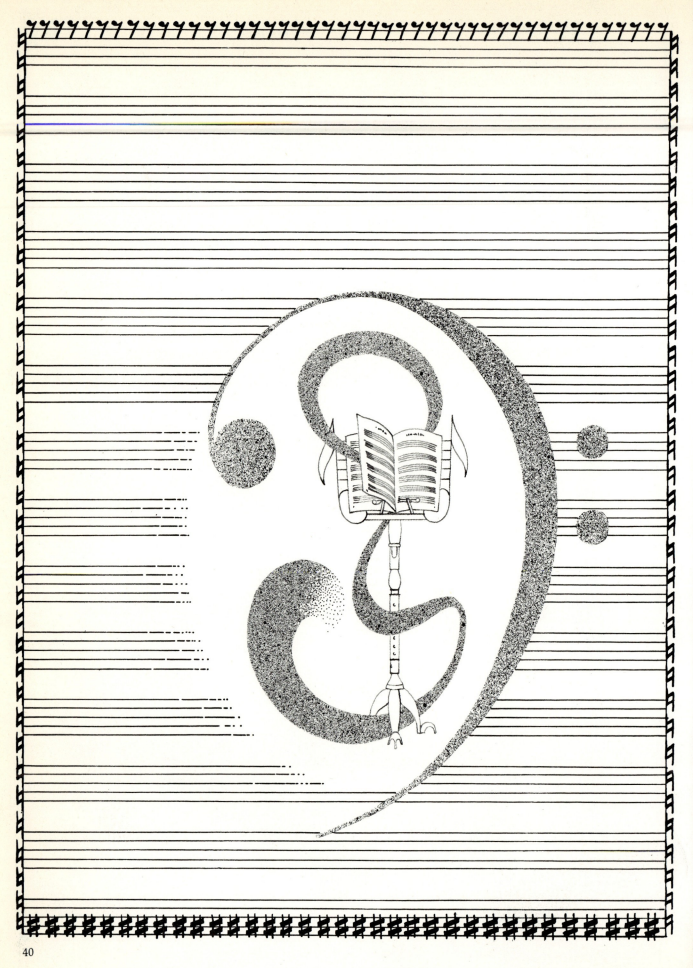

Mister Frog

(Quick ♩)

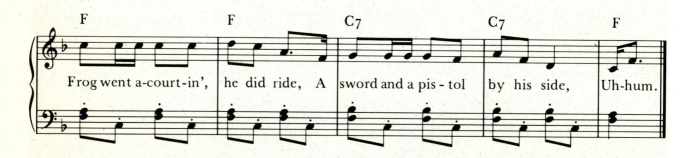

1. Mister Frog went a-courtin', he did ride, Uh – hum,
   Mister Frog went a-courtin', he did ride,
   A sword and pistol by his side, Uh – hum.

2. He rode up to Lady Mousie's door, Uh – hum,
   He rode up to Lady Mousie's door,
   He knocked and knocked till his thumb got sore, Uh – hum.

3. He took Lady Mousie on his knee, Uh – hum,
   He took Lady Mousie on his knee,
   Said he, 'Lady Mouse will you marry me?' Uh – hum.

4. Oh, where shall the wedding supper be? Uh – hum,
   Oh, where shall the wedding supper be?
   Way down yonder in a hollow tree, Uh – hum.

5 Oh, what shall the wedding supper be? Uh – hum,
   Oh, what shall the wedding supper be?
   Two blue beans and a black-eyed pea, Uh – hum.

6 Then Frog come a-swimmin' across the lake, Uh – hum,
   Then Frog come a-swimmin' across the lake,
   Got swallowed up by a big black snake, Uh – hum.

SHORT'NIN' BREAD

1. Three little chillun, lyin' in bed,
   Two was sick and the other 'most dead.
   Sent for the doctor, doctor said,
   'Feed those chillun on short'nin' bread.'
   Mama's little baby loves short'nin', short'nin',
   Mama's little baby loves short'nin' bread,
   Mama's little baby loves short'nin' bread.

2 When them chillun sick in bed,
 Heard that talk about short'nin' bread,
 Popped up well to dance and sing,
 Skipped around, cut the pigeon wing.
   Chorus

3 I slipped in the kitchen, I raised up the lid,
 I stole me a mess of that short'nin' bread.
 I winked at the pretty gal and I said,
 'Baby, how'd you like some short'nin' bread?'
   Chorus

4 They caught me with the skillet, caught me with the lid,
 Caught me with that gal making short'nin' bread.
 Six months for the skillet, six months for the lid,
 Now I'm doin' time for eatin' short'nin' bread.
   Chorus

1 *Jim crack corn, I don't care,*
Jim crack corn, I don't care,
Jim crack corn, I don't care,
Ole Massa's gone away.

2 When I was young I used to wait
  On Massa an' hand him de plate,
  An' pass de bottle when he git dry
  An' brush away de blue-tail fly.
                              Chorus

3 An' when he ride in de arternoon,
  I foller wid a hickory broom,
  De pony being very shy,
  When bitten by de blue-tail fly.
                              Chorus

4 One day he ride aroun' de farm,
  De flies so numerous dey did swarm.
  One chance to bite 'im on de thigh,
  De Devil take dat blue-tail fly.
                              Chorus

5 De pony run, he jump an' pitch,
  An' tumble Massa in de ditch.
  He died, de jury wondered why;
  De verdict was de blue-tail fly.
                              Chorus

6 Dey laid 'im under a 'simmon tree,
  His epitaph is dar to see:
  'Beneath dis stone I'm forced to lie,
  All by de means of de blue-tail fly.'
                              Chorus

Shanghai Chicken

(Fast ♩)

Shang-hai chick-en an' he grow so tall, Hoo-day! Hoo-day!
Take that egg a month to fall, Hoo-day! Hoo-day!

Shanghai chicken an' he grow so tall,
Hooday! Hooday!
Take that egg a month to fall,
Hooday! Hooday!

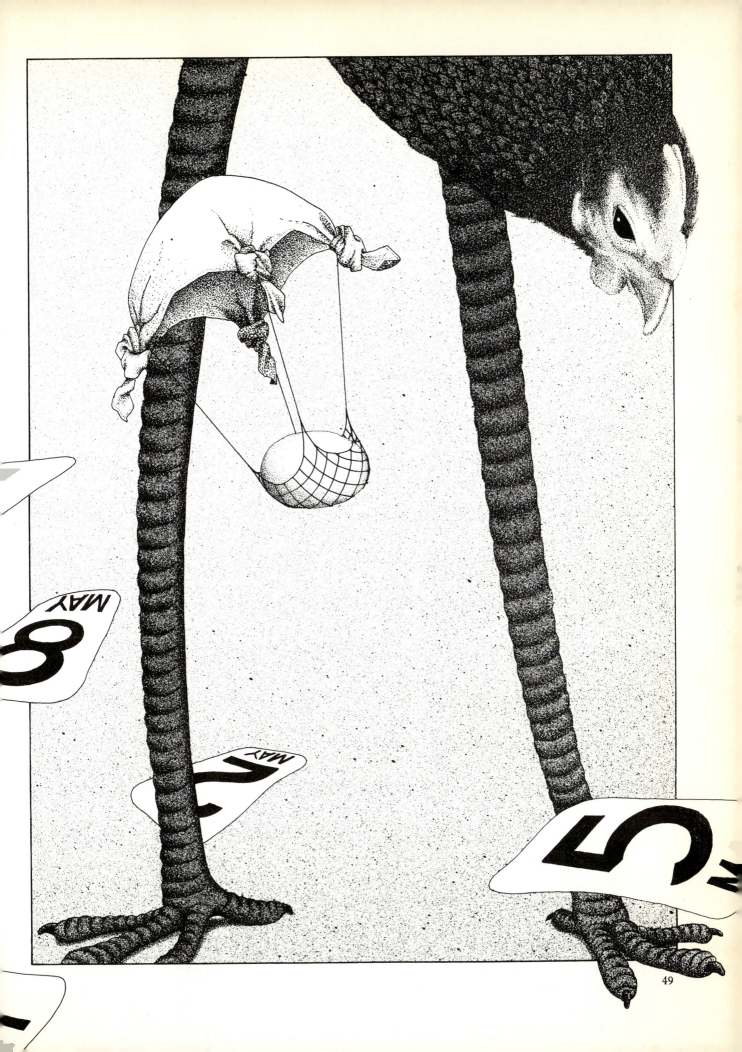

Bullfrog

1. Bullfrog jumped in de middle of de spring,
   An' I ain't a-going to weep no mo'.
   He tied his tail to a hick'ry limb,
   An' I ain't a-going to weep no mo'.

   Fare ye well, my ladies,
   I'll join dat heavenly band,
   Where dere ain't any weepin' any mo'.
   Fare ye well, my ladies,
   I'll join dat heavenly band,
   Where dere ain't any weepin' any mo'.

2. He kicked an' he rared an' he couldn't make a jump,
   An' I ain't a-going to weep no mo'.
   He kicked an' he rared an' he couldn't make a jump,
   An' I ain't a-going to weep no mo'.
   Chorus

The Train is A-Coming

1 The train is a-coming, oh yes!
   Train is a-coming, oh yes!
   Train is a-coming, train is a-coming,
   Train is a-coming, oh yes!

2 Better buy your ticket, oh yes!
   Better buy your ticket, oh yes!
   Better buy your ticket, better buy your ticket,
   Better buy your ticket, oh yes!

3 King Jesus is conductor, oh yes!
   King Jesus is conductor, oh yes!
   King Jesus is conductor, King Jesus is conductor,
   King Jesus is conductor, oh yes!

1 First He made a sun, then He made a moon
  Then He made a possum, then He made a coon.
  All the other creatures, He made 'em one by one,
  Stuck 'em on the fence to dry as soon as they was done.
      Walk-ee-in, walk-ee-in,
      Walk in I say.
      Walk into the parlour
      And hear the banjo play.
      Walk into the parlour
      And hear the Negroes sing,
      And watch the Negro's fingers
      As he picks upon the string.
          Zing, zing, zing, zing,
          Zing, zing, zing.

2 Old Mother Eve
  Couldn't sleep without a pillow,
  And the greatest man that ever lived
  Was Jack the Giant-killer.
                    Refrain

3 Old Noah, he was a mighty man
  And built a mighty ark,
  And got all the creatures in
  Just before the dark.
                    Refrain

THE OLD GREY GOOSE

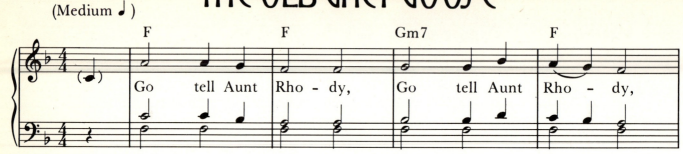

1 Go tell Aunt Rhody,
go tell Aunt Rhody,
go tell Aunt Rhody
the old grey goose is dead.

2 The one that she's been saving,
the one that she's been saving,
the one that she's been saving
to make a feather bed.

3 She died in the mill pond,
she died in the mill pond,
she died in the mill pond
a-standing on her head.

4 The goslings are crying,
the goslings are crying,
the goslings are crying
because their mammy's dead.

What's Little Babies Made Of?

(Fast ♩)

What's lit-tle ba-bies made of, made of, O what's lit-tle ba-bies made of?
Cry and suck and to be pet-ted up, And that's what lit-tle ba-bies made of.

1 What's little babies made of, made of,
   O what's little babies made of?
   Cry and suck and to be petted up,
   And that's what little babies made of.

2 What's little boys made of, etc.
   Bows and arrows to shoot little sparrows,
   And that's what little boys made of.

3 What's little girls made of, etc.
   Ribbons and rings and all pretty things,
   And that's what little girls made of.

4 What's young ladies made of, etc.
   Sugar and sop and sweet rosy top,
   And that's what young ladies made of.

5 What's young men made of, etc.
   Thorns and briars, they're all bad liars,
   And that's what young men made of.

6 What's old women made of, etc.
   Moans and groans in their old aching bones,
   And that's what old women made of.

7 What's old men made of, etc.
   Go to town to spend their crown,
   And that's what old men made of.

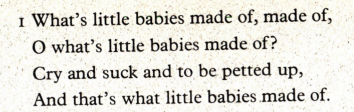

59

Mister Rabbit

(Steady ♩)

1 Mister Rabbit, Mister Rabbit, yo' ears mighty long.
Yes, my lawd, dey're put on wrong!
Ev'ry little soul must shine, shine, shine,
Ev'ry little soul must shine, shine, shine.

2 Mister Rabbit, Mister Rabbit, yo' coat mighty grey.
Yes, my lawd, 'twas made dat way.
Ev'ry little soul must shine, shine, shine,
Ev'ry little soul must shine, shine, shine.

3 Mister Rabbit, Mister Rabbit, yo' feet mighty red.
  Yes, my lawd, I'm a-almost dead.
    Ev'ry little soul must shine, shine, shine,
    Ev'ry little soul must shine, shine, shine.

4 Mister Rabbit, Mister Rabbit, yo' tail mighty white.
  Yes, my lawd, an' I'm gittin' out o' sight.
    Ev'ry little soul must shine, shine, shine,
    Ev'ry little soul must shine, shine, shine.

1. Little bird, little bird, go through my window,
   Little bird, little bird, go through my window,
   Little bird, little bird, go through my window,
   And buy molasses candy.
   > Go through my window, my sugar lump,
   > Go through my window, my sugar lump,
   > And buy molasses candy.

2. Blue bird, blue bird, go through my window,
   Blue bird, blue bird, go through my window,
   Blue bird, blue bird, go through my window,
   And buy molasses candy.
   > Go through my window, my little bird,
   > Go through my window, my little bird,
   > And buy molasses candy.

A Little Boy Threw His Ball

(Leisurely ♩.)

1. A little boy threw his ball so high,
   He threw his ball so low.
   He threw it into a dusky garden
   Among the blades of snow.

2 'Come hither, come hither, my sweet little boy,
   Come hither and get your ball.'
  'I'll neither come hither, I'll neither come there,
   I'll not come to get my ball.'

3 She showed him an apple as yellow as gold,
   She showed him a bright gold ring,
  She showed him a cherry as red as blood,
   And that enticed him in.

4 Enticed him into the drawing-room,
   And then into the kitchen,
  And there he saw his own dear nurse
   A' pi-i-icking a chicken!

The Mermaid

(Flowing ♩)

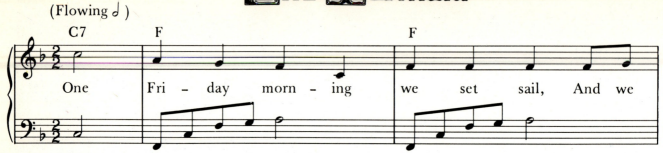

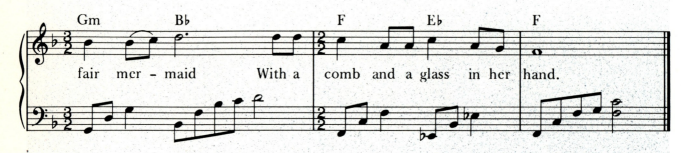

1 One Friday morning we set sail,
And we hadn't got far from land,
Till there I spied a fair mermaid
With a comb and a glass in her hand.
And stormy winds may blow, blow, blow,
And the raging seas may flow,
While it's us poor sailors a-climbing to the top
And the landsmen lying down below.

2 It's up said the captain of our gallant ship,
　And a well-looking man was he.
　I've a child and a wife in my own native land,
　This night she a widow may be.
　　And the stormy winds may blow, etc.

3 Then three times round went our gallant ship,
　And three times around went she.
　And the third time that she sailed around,
　She sank to the bottom of the sea.
　　And the stormy winds may blow, etc.

Old Ponto is Dead

(Steady 𝅗𝅥.)

1. Old Ponto is dead and laid in his grave,
   Laid in his grave, laid in his grave.
   Old Ponto is dead and laid in his grave.
   Whoo! whoo! whoo!

2. There grew a large apple tree over his grave,
   Over his grave, over his grave.
   There grew a large apple tree over his grave.
   Whoo! whoo! whoo!

3. The apples got ripe and ready to fall,
   Ready to fall, ready to fall.
   The apples got ripe and ready to fall.
   Whoo! whoo! whoo!

4 There came an old woman picking them up,
　Picking them up, picking them up.
　There came an old woman picking them up.
　　　Whoo! whoo! whoo!

5 Old Ponto jumped up and gave her a thump,
　Gave her a thump, gave her a thump.
　Old Ponto jumped up and gave her a thump.
　　　Whoo! whoo! whoo!

6 It made the old woman go hippity-hop,
　Hippity-hop, hippity-hop.
　It made the old woman go hippity-hop.
　　　Whoo! whoo! whoo!

The American Stranger

1 I'm a stranger in this country,
   From America I came.
   There is no one that knows me,
   Nor can tell me my name.
   I have wandered from my darling
   A many long mile.

2 Some says I am ragged,
   More says I am wild.
   Some says I am foolish,
   My mind to beguile.
   But to prove myself loyal,
   You should come along with me,
   And I'll take you to America,
   My darling to be.

3 The moon shall be in darkness
   And the sun give no light,
   If ever I prove false
   To my own heart's delight.
   In the middle of the ocean
   There shall grow a myrtle tree,
   If ever I prove false
   To the girl that loves me.

1 My name was Robert Kidd,
As I sailed, as I sailed,
My name was Robert Kidd,
As I sailed.
My name was Robert Kidd
And God's laws I did forbid,
And much wickedness I did,
As I sailed, as I sailed,
And much wickedness I did,
As I sailed.

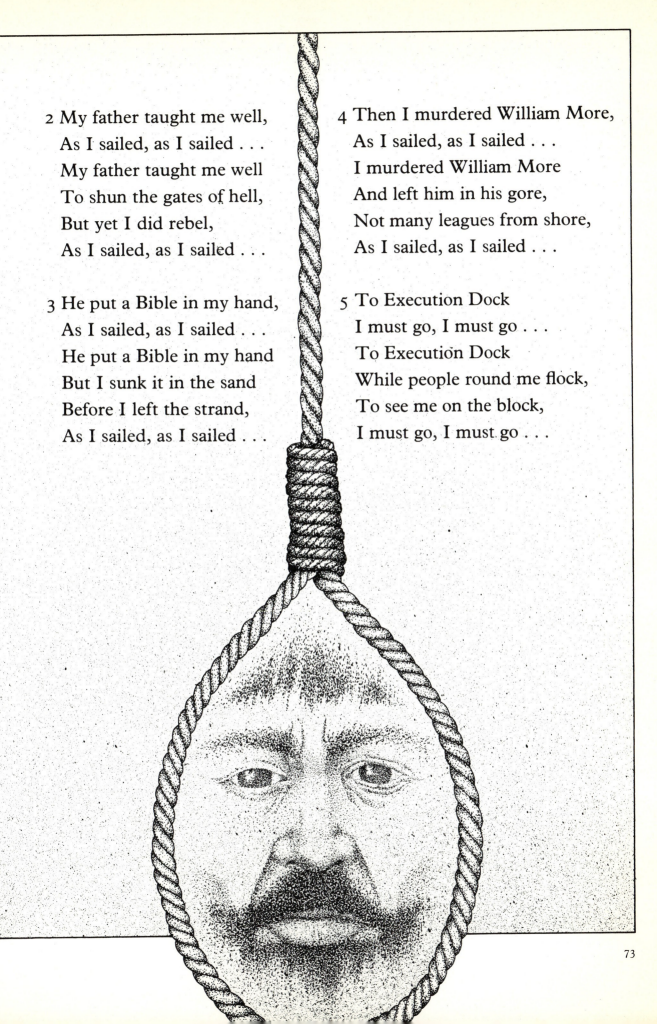

2 My father taught me well,
   As I sailed, as I sailed . . .
   My father taught me well
   To shun the gates of hell,
   But yet I did rebel,
   As I sailed, as I sailed . . .

3 He put a Bible in my hand,
   As I sailed, as I sailed . . .
   He put a Bible in my hand
   But I sunk it in the sand
   Before I left the strand,
   As I sailed, as I sailed . . .

4 Then I murdered William More,
   As I sailed, as I sailed . . .
   I murdered William More
   And left him in his gore,
   Not many leagues from shore,
   As I sailed, as I sailed . . .

5 To Execution Dock
   I must go, I must go . . .
   To Execution Dock
   While people round me flock,
   To see me on the block,
   I must go, I must go . . .

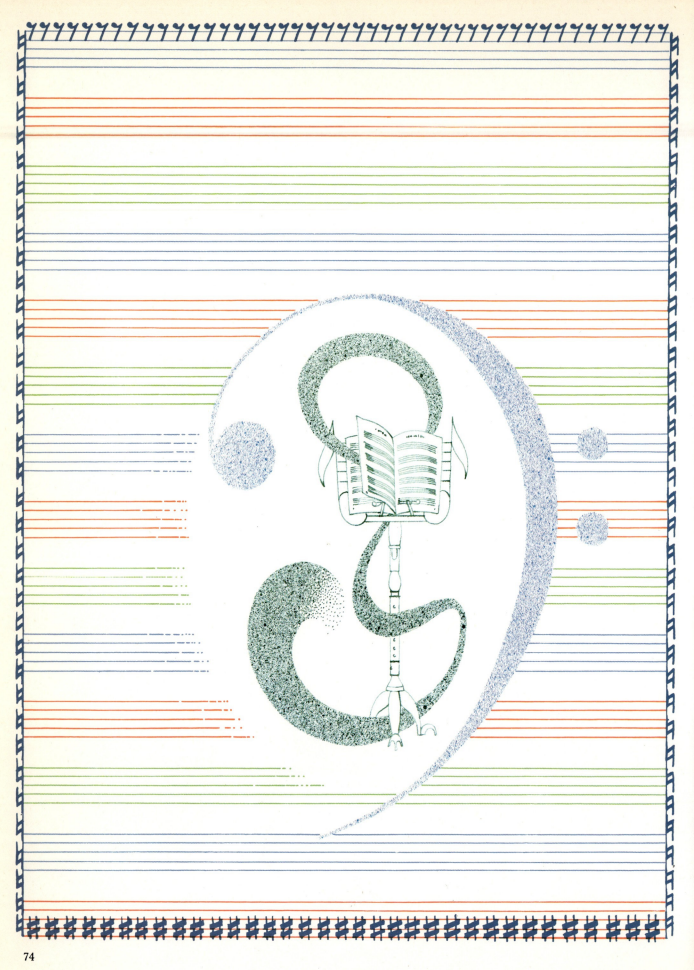

The Hunt is Up

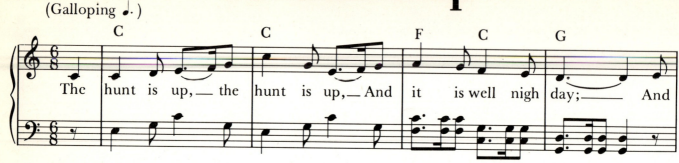

1 The hunt is up, the hunt is up,
And it is well nigh day;
And Harry our king is gone hunting
To bring his deer to bay.

2 The east is bright with morning light,
And darkness it is fled.
And the merry horn wakes up the morn
To leave his idle bed.

3 The sun is glad to see us clad
All in our lusty green,
And smiles in the sky as he rises high,
To see and to be seen.

4 Awake all men, I say again,
Be merry as you may;
For Harry our king is gone hunting
To bring his deer to bay.

The Maid and the Miller

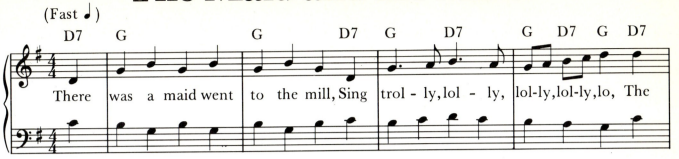

1 There was a maid went to the mill,
   Sing trolly, lolly, lolly, lolly, lo,
   The mill turned round, but the maid stood still,
   Oh, oh, ho! oh, oh, ho! oh, oh, ho! said she so?

2 The miller he kissed her, away she went,
   Sing trolly, etc.
   The maid was well pleased, and the miller content,
   Oh, oh, ho! oh, oh, ho! oh, oh, ho! was it so?

3 He danced and he sang while the mill went clack,
   Sing trolly, etc.
   And he cherished his heart with a cup of old sack,
   Oh, oh, ho! oh, oh, ho! oh, oh, ho! did he so?

There was an old woman tossed up in a basket
Seventeen times as high as the moon.
Where she was going, I could not but ask it,
For in her hand she carried a broom.
'Old woman, old woman, old woman,' said I,
'O whither, O whither, O whither so high?'
'To sweep the cobwebs from the sky,
But I'll be with you by and by.'

1 A hungry fox one day did spy,
    Fal lal la, la la la la la,
Some nice ripe grapes that hung so high,
    Fal lal la, la la la la la,
And as they hung they seemed to say
To him who underneath did stay,
'If you can fetch me down you may.'
    Fal lal la, la la la la la.

2 The fox his patience nearly lost,
    Fal lal la, etc.
With expectations baulked and crossed,
    Fal lal la, etc.
He licked his lips for near an hour,
Till he found the prize beyond his power,
Then he went, and swore the grapes were sour!
    Fal lal la, etc.

There was a Monkey Climbed Up a Tree

1 There was a monkey climbed up a tree,
When he fell down, then down fell he.
There was a crow sat on a stone,
When he was gone, then there was none.
There was an old wife did eat an apple,
When she'd eat two, she'd eat a couple.

2 There was a horse going to the mill,
When he went on, he stood not still.
There was a butcher cut his thumb,
When it did bleed, the blood did come.
There was a navy went into Spain,
When it returned it came back again.

The Sluggard

1 'Tis the voice of the sluggard, I heard him complain,
'You have waked me too soon, I must slumber again.'
As the door on its hinges, so he on his bed,
Turns his sides and his shoulders, and his heavy head.

2 'A little more sleep, a little more slumber,'
  He wastes all his days and his hours without number,
  And when he gets up he sits folding his hands,
  Or walks about saunt'ring, or trifling, he stands.

3 I passed by his garden and saw the wild briar,
  The thorn and the thistle grow broader and higher;
  The clothes that hang on him are turnèd to rags,
  His money he wastes, till he starves or he begs.

4 Said I then to my heart, 'Here's a lesson to me,
  That man's but a picture of what I might be.
  But thanks to my friends for their care in my breeding,
  Who taught me in time to love working and reading.'

THREE JOVIAL WELSHMEN

(Fast ♩.)

1 There were three jovial Welshmen, as I have heard them say,
  And they would go a-hunting, upon Saint David's Day.

2 All day they hunted and nothing they could find,
  But a ship a-sailing, and that they left behind.
  One said it was a ship, the other he said 'Nay,'
  The third one said it was a house with chimney blown away.

3 All the night they hunted and nothing could they find,
   But the moon a-gliding, and that they left behind.
   One said it was the moon, the other he said 'Nay,'
   The third one said it was a cheese with half cut away.

4 All day they hunted and nothing could they find,
   But a hedgehog in a bramble, and that they left behind.
   One said it was a hedgehog, the other he said 'Nay,'
   The third one said a pin-cushion with pins stuck in wrong way.

5 All the night they hunted and nothing could they find,
   But an owl in a holly bush, and that they left behind.
   One said it was an owl, the other he said 'Nay,'
   The third one said it was a man with a beard growing grey.

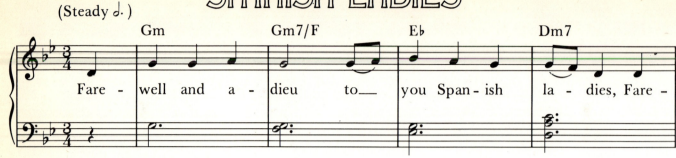

Farewell and adieu to you Spanish ladies,
Farewell and adieu to you ladies of Spain,
For we've received orders to sail for old England,
But I hope in short time we shall see you again.

DR FAUSTUS

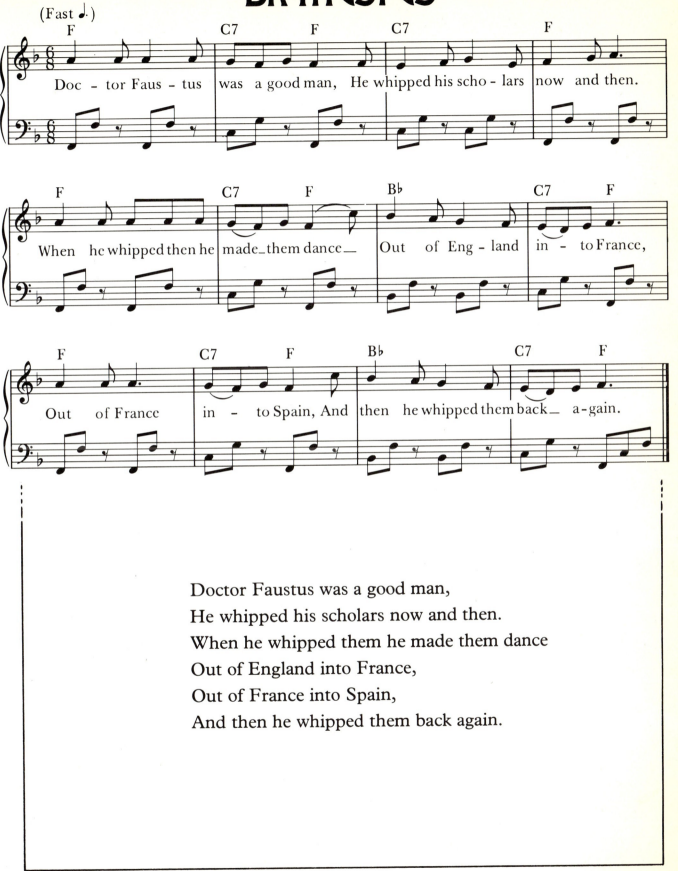

Doctor Faustus was a good man,

He whipped his scholars now and then.

When he whipped them he made them dance

Out of England into France,

Out of France into Spain,

And then he whipped them back again.

Tom the Piper's Son

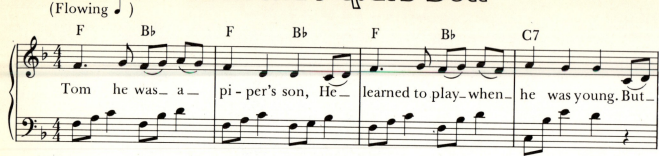

1. Tom he was a piper's son,
   He learned to play when he was young.
   But all the tunes that he could play
   Was 'O'er the hills and far away'.

2. Tom went piping down the street,
   And every one that he did meet,
   Put down their work to hear him play
   'O'er the hills and far away'.

3. The oxen stood and gazed at him,
   They thought it such a funny whim.
   The ass let out a tuneful bray,
   At 'O'er the hills and far away'.

4. Dolly a-milking of her cow,
   She let it loose, I don't know how,
   Who kicked the milk and ran away
   'O'er the hills and far away'.

The Fox and the Goose

(Fast ♪)

1 The fox went out one moonlight night,
   He begged the moon to give some light,
   For he had a long way for to go
   Before he do return O, return O, return O,
   For he had a long way for to go
   Before he do return O.

2 The fox went through the farmer's yard,
   The ducks and the geese were all afraid,
   He said, 'The best of you shall grease my beard
   Before I do return O,' etc, etc.

3 Old mother Widdy Waddy jumped out of bed,
   And out of the window she popped her head,
   Saying, 'Run, John, run, the grey goose has gone
   And the fox is on the town O,' etc, etc.

4 The fox he came into his den,
   There were the young ones nine or ten.
   He cut up the goose without any knife,
   And the young ones had the bones O, etc, etc.

How Doth the Little Busy Bee

1. How doth the little busy bee
   Improve each shining hour.
   And gather honey all the day
   From ev'ry op'ning flower.

2. How skilfully she builds her cell,
   How neat she spreads the wax.
   And labours hard to store it well,
   With the sweet food she makes.

3. In works of labour or of skill,
   I would be busy too.
   For Satan finds some mischief still
   For idle hands to do.

4. In books, or work, or healthful play,
   Let my first years be passed.
   That I might give for every day,
   Some good account at last.

Sing Ivy

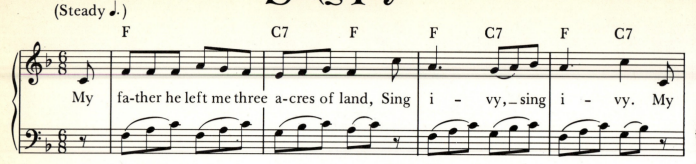

1 My father he left me three acres of land,
   Sing ivy, sing ivy.
My father he left me three acres of land,
   Sing holly, go whistle and ivy.

2 I ploughed it one morning with a ram's horn,
   Sing ivy, etc.
And sowed it all over with one pepper corn,
   Sing holly, etc.

3 I harrowed it next with a bramble bush,
   Sing ivy, etc.
And reaped it all with my little penknife,
   Sing holly, etc.

4 The mice for me carried it into the barn,
   Sing ivy, etc.
  And there I threshed it with a goose quill,
   Sing holly, etc.

5 The cat she carried it into the mill,
   Sing ivy, sing ivy.
  And the miller he said that he'd work with a will,
   Sing holly, go whistle and ivy.

My Boy Willie

1 O where have you been all the day, my boy Willie?
O where have you been all the day?
O Willie won't you tell me now?
I've been all the day, courting of a lady gay,
But she is too young to be taken from her mammy.

2 Can she brew and can she bake, my boy Willie?
  O can she brew and can she bake?
  O Willie won't you tell me now?
  She can brew and she can bake, and she can make a wedding cake,
  But she is too young to be taken from her mammy.

3 Can she knit and can she spin, my boy Willie?
  O can she knit and can she spin?
  O Willie won't you tell me now?
  She can knit and she can spin, she can do most anything,
  But she is too young to be taken from her mammy.

4 How old is she now, my boy Willie?
  O how old is she now?
  O Willie won't you tell me now?
  Twice six, twice seven, twice twenty and eleven,
  But she is too young to be taken from her mammy.

Scarborough Fair

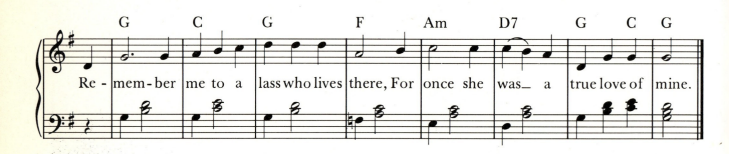

1. O, where are you going? To Scarborough Fair,
   Savoury sage, rosemary and thyme;
   Remember me to a lass who lives there,
   For once she was a true love of mine.

2. And tell her to make me a cambric shirt,
   Savoury sage, rosemary and thyme,
   Without any seam or needlework,
   And then she shall be a true love of mine.

3. And tell her to wash it in yonder dry well,
   Savoury sage, rosemary and thyme,
   Where no water sprung, nor a drop of rain fell,
   And then she shall be a true love of mine.

4 O, will you find me an acre of land,
　Savoury sage, rosemary and thyme,
　Between the sea foam and the sea sand,
　Or never be a true love of mine.

5 O, will you plough it with a ram's horn,
　Savoury sage, rosemary and thyme,
　And sow it all over with one peppercorn,
　Or never be a true love of mine.

Adieu to Old England

(Gently swinging ♩.)

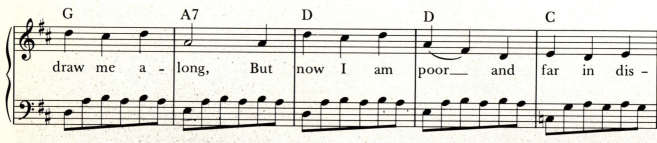
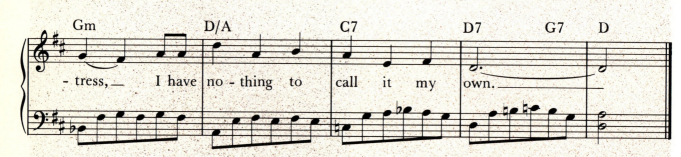

1. O once I could ride in my coach
   And horses to draw me along,
   But now I am poor and far in distress,
   I have nothing to call it my own.
   Adieu to old England, adieu,
   Adieu to some hundred of pounds.
   If the world had been ended when I was young,
   My sorrows I should never have known.

2 O once I could eat of the best,
   The bestest of bread so brown,
   But now I am glad for the hard mouldy crust
   And glad I could swallow it down.
   Refrain

3 O once I could drink of the best,
   The bestest of ale so brown,
   But now I am glad with a cup of cold water
   That runneth from town to town.
   Refrain

4 O once I could lie on my bed,
   My bed was the softest of down,
   But now I am glad of a bale of clean straw
   To keep me from the hard ground.
   Refrain

Three Maidens A-Milking Did Go

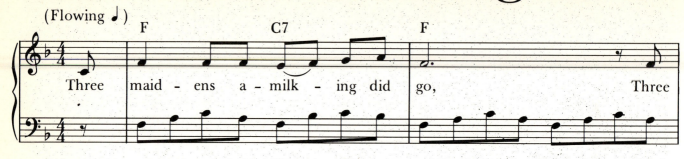

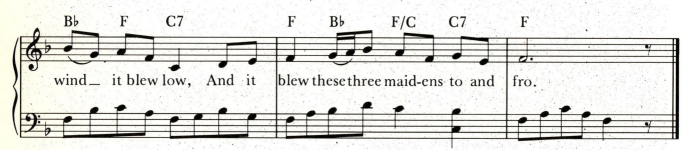

Three maidens a-milking did go,
Three maidens a-milking did go;
The wind it blew high, and the wind it blew low,
And it blew these three maidens to and fro.

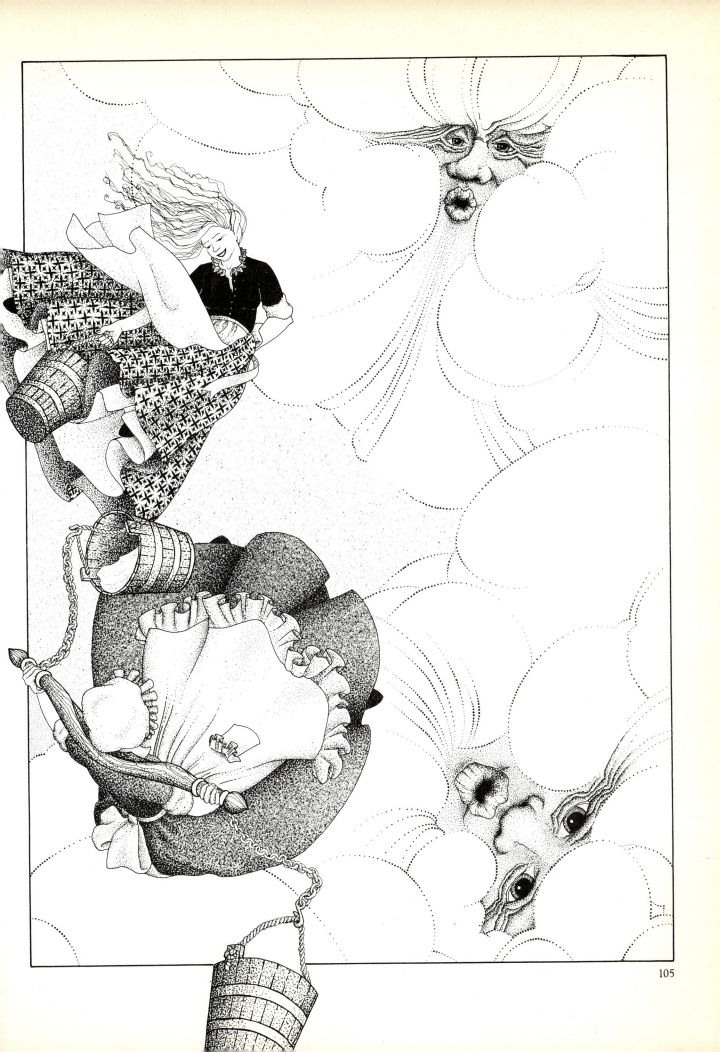

1 Yankee doodle came to town,
   Riding on a pony,
   He stuck a feather in his cap
   And called it macaroni.
   Yankee doodle, doodle do,
   Yankee doodle dandy.
   All the lassies are so smart,
   And sweet as sugar candy.

2 Marching in and marching out,
   And marching round the town, O.
   Here there comes a regiment
   With Captain Thomas Brown, O.
   Yankee doodle, etc.

3 Yankee doodle is a tune
   That comes in mighty handy.
   The enemy all runs away
   At Yankee doodle dandy.
   Yankee doodle, etc.

The Holly and the Ivy

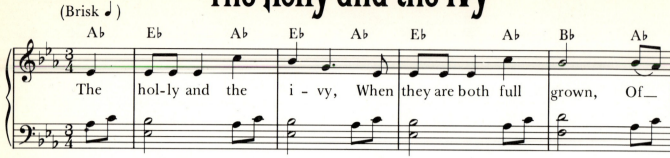
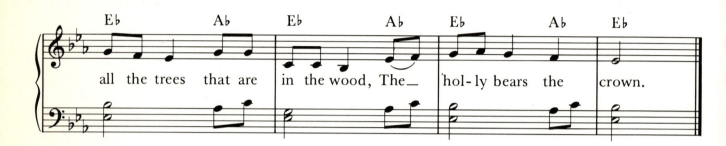

1 The holly and the ivy,
   When they are both full grown,
   Of all the trees that are in the wood,
   The holly bears the crown.

2 The holly bears a blossom,
   As white as the lily flower,
   And Mary bore sweet Jesus Christ,
   To be our sweet Saviour.

3 The holly bears a berry,
   As red as any blood,
   And Mary bore sweet Jesus Christ
   To do us sinners good.

4 The holly bears a prickle,
   As sharp as any thorn,
   And Mary bore sweet Jesus Christ
   On Christmas day in the morn.

5 The holly bears a bark,
   As bitter as any gall,
   And Mary bore sweet Jesus Christ
   For to redeem us all.

As I Sat on a Sunny Bank

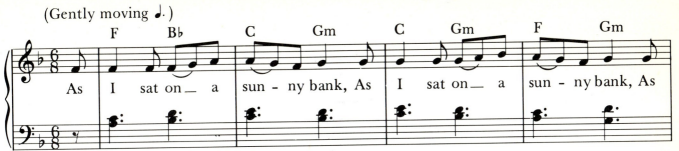

1 As I sat on a sunny bank,
   As I sat on a sunny bank,
   As I sat on a sunny bank,
   On Christmas Day all in the morning.

2 I saw three ships come sailing home,
   I saw three ships come sailing home,
   I saw three ships come sailing home,
   On Christmas Day all in the morning.

3 Who do you think were in those ships?
   Who do you think were in those ships?
   Who do you think were in those ships?
   On Christmas Day all in the morning.

4 Christ and His Mother were in those ships,
   Christ and His Mother were in those ships,
   Christ and His Mother were in those ships,
   On Christmas Day all in the morning.

The Bitter Withy

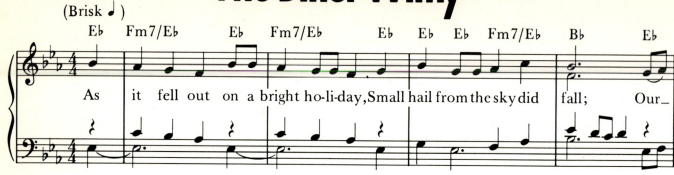

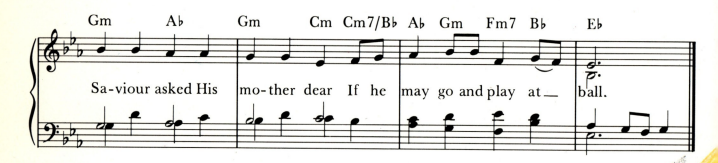

1. As it fell out on a bright holiday,
   Small hail from the sky did fall;
   Our Saviour asked His mother dear
   If he may go and play at ball.

2. So up Lincull and down Lincull
   Our sweetest Saviour ran,
   And there He met three rich young lords:
   Good morning to you all.

3. We are lords' and ladies' sons,
   Born in a bower and hall;
   And Thou art nothing but a poor maid's child,
   Born in an ox's stall.

4 So He made Him a bridge with the beams of the sun,
   And o'er the water crossed He.
   The rich young lords followed after Him,
   And drowned they were all three.

5 So Mary mild fetched home her child,
   And laid Him across her knee;
   With a handful of green withy twigs
   She gave Him slashes three.

6 O withy, O withy, O bitter withy!
   Thou hast caused Me to smart,
   And the withy shall be the very first tree
   That shall perish at the heart.

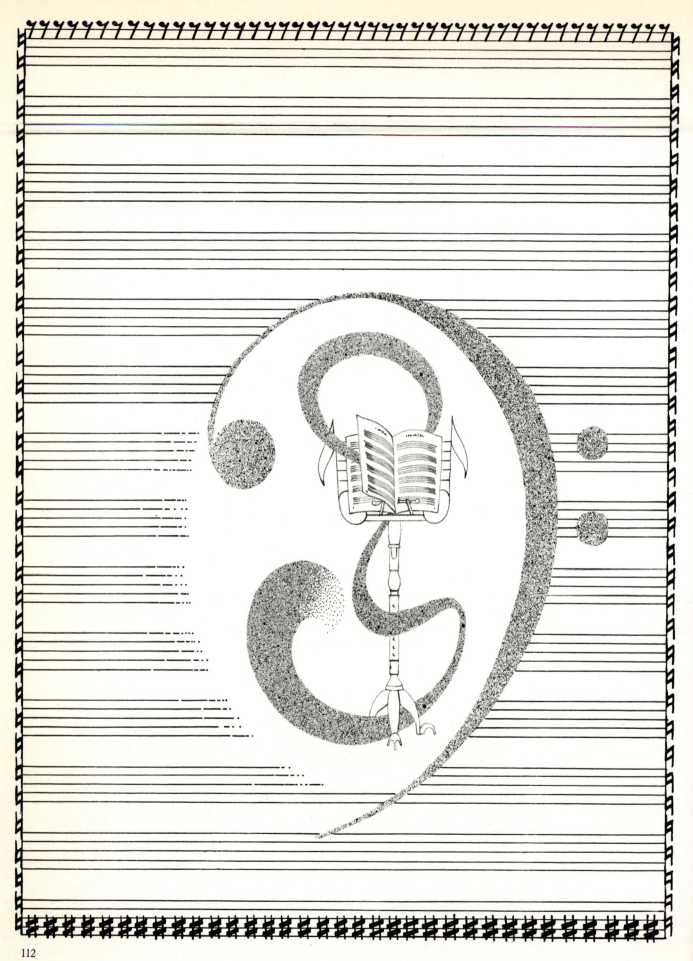

1 O dear what can the matter be?
O! what can the matter be?
Dear! what can the matter be?
Johnny's so long at the fair.
He promised he'd buy me a fairing should please me,
And then, for a kiss, O he vowed he would tease me,
He promised he'd bring me a bunch of blue ribbons
 To tie up my bonny brown hair.

2 O dear what can the matter be?
Dear, dear what can the matter be?
O dear what can the matter be?
Johnny's so long at the fair.
He promised to buy me a pair of sleeve buttons,
A pair of new garters that cost him but tuppence,
He promised he'd bring me a bunch of blue ribbons
 To tie up my bonny brown hair.

3 O dear what can the matter be?
Dear, dear what can the matter be?
O dear what can the matter be?
Johnny's so long at the fair.
He promised he'd bring me a basket of posies,
A garland of lilies, a garland of roses,
A little straw hat to set off the blue ribbons
 To tie up my bonny brown hair.

1 Cold blows the wind from east to west,
  The drift is driving fairly.
  So loud and shrill I hear the blast,
  I'm sure it's winter fairly.
   Up in the morning's no for me,
   Up in the morning early,
   When a' the hills are cover'd with snow,
   I'm sure it is winter fairly.

2 The birds sit chittering in the thorn,
  To-day they fare but sparely;
  And long's the night from eve to morn,
  I'm sure it's winter fairly.
   Up in the morning's no for me, etc.

AULD KING COLE

(Fast ♩)

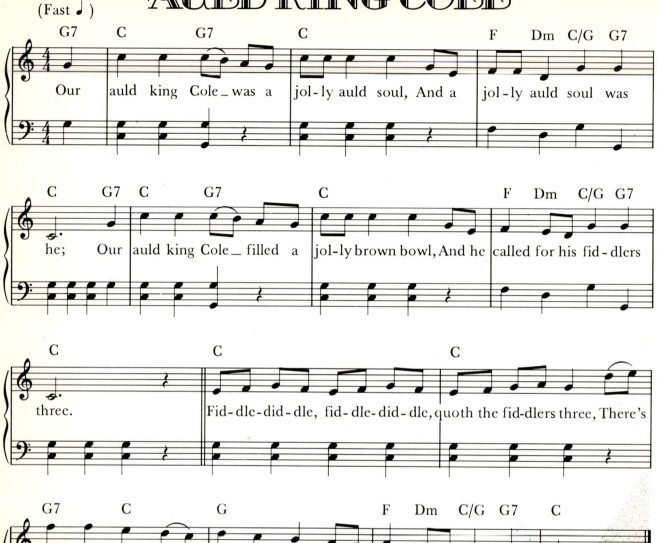

1 Our auld king Cole was a jolly auld soul,
And a jolly auld soul was he;
Our auld kind Cole filled a jolly brown bowl,
And he called for his fiddlers three.
Fiddle-diddle, fiddle-diddle, quoth the fiddlers three,
There's not a lass in all Scotland
Like our sweet Marjorie.

2 Our auld king Cole was a jolly auld soul,
And a jolly auld soul was he;
Our auld king Cole filled a jolly brown bowl,
And he called for his pipers three.
Ha-diddle, ho-diddle, quoth the pipers,
Fiddle-diddle, fiddle-diddle, quoth the fiddlers three,
There's not a lass in all Scotland
Like our sweet Marjorie.

3 Our auld king Cole was a jolly auld soul,
And a jolly auld soul was he;
Our auld king Cole filled a jolly brown bowl,
And he called for his drummers three.
Rub-a-dub, rub-a-dub, quoth the drummers,
Ha-diddle, ho-diddle, quoth the pipers,
Fiddle-diddle, fiddle-diddle, quoth the fiddlers three,
There's not a lass in all Scotland
Like our sweet Marjorie.

Rattling, Roaring Willie

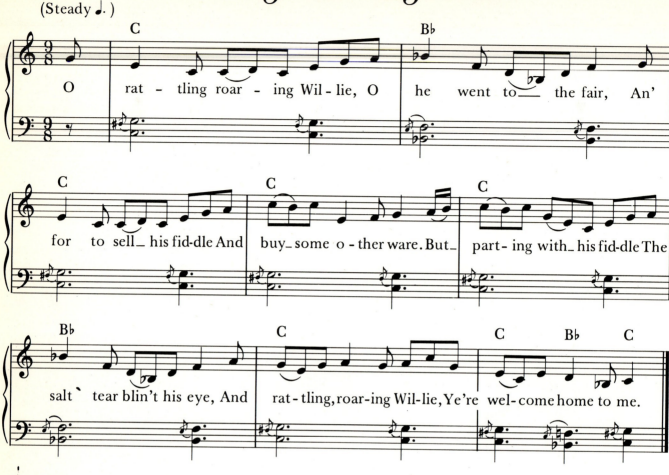

1 O rattling, roaring Willie,
   O he went to the fair,
   An' for to sell his fiddle
   And buy some other ware.
   But parting with his fiddle
   The salt tear blin't his eye,
   And rattling, roaring Willie,
   Ye're welcome home to me.

2 O Willie, come sell your fiddle,
   O sell your fiddle so fine;
   O Willie, come sell your fiddle
   And buy a pint o' wine.
   If I should sell my fiddle,
   The world would think I was mad,
   For many a ranting day
   My fiddle and I have had.

If I was a Blackbird

1 If I was a blackbird I'd whistle and sing
And I'd follow the ship that my true love sails in,
And on the top riggings I'd there build my nest,
And I'd pillow my head on his lily-white breast.

2 I am a young maid and my story is sad,
For once I was courted by a brave sailor lad.
He courted me strongly by night and by day,
But now my dear sailor is gone far away.
If I was a blackbird, etc.

3 His parents they slight me and will not agree
That I and my sailor boy married should be.
But when he comes home I will greet him with joy,
And I'll take to my bosom my dear sailor boy.
If I was a blackbird, etc.

The Kerry Recruit

(Swinging ♩.)

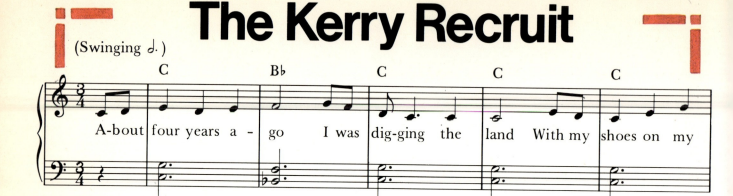

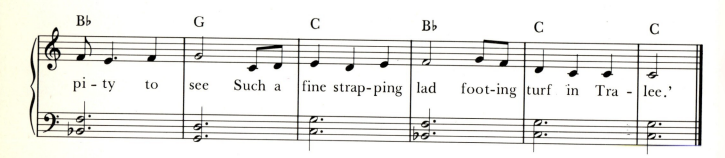

1 About four years ago I was digging the land
   With my shoes on my feet and my spade in my hand.
   Says I to myself 'What a pity to see
   Such a fine strapping lad footing turf in Tralee.'

2 So I buttered my shoes and shook hands with my spade,
   And I went to the fair like a dashing young blade,
   When up comes a sergeant and asks me to 'list,
   'Arrah, sergeant a gra, put the bob in my fist.'

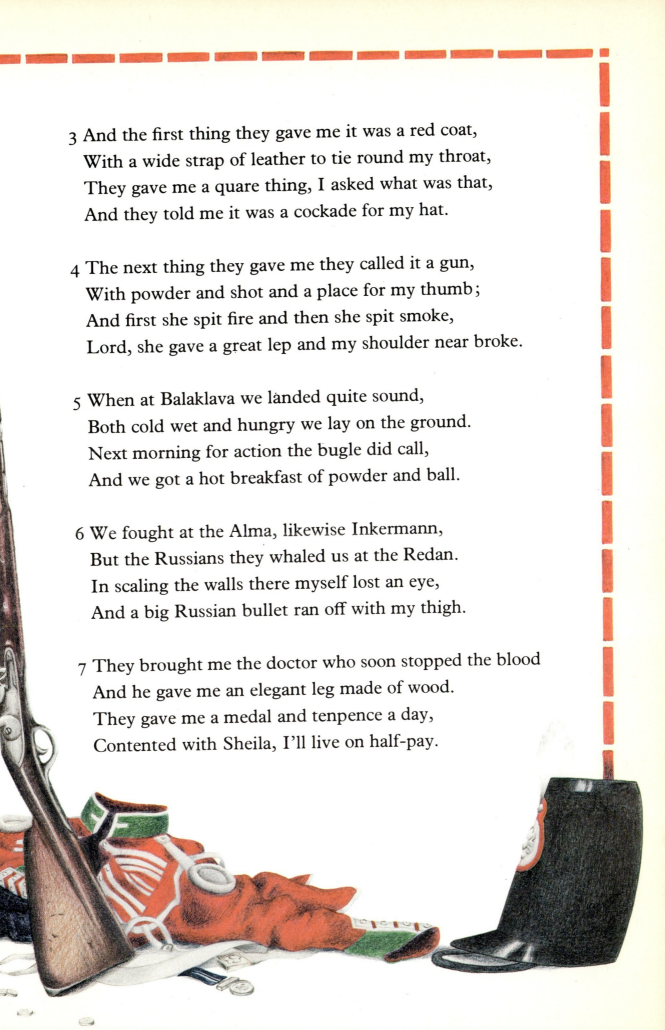

3 And the first thing they gave me it was a red coat,
   With a wide strap of leather to tie round my throat,
   They gave me a quare thing, I asked what was that,
   And they told me it was a cockade for my hat.

4 The next thing they gave me they called it a gun,
   With powder and shot and a place for my thumb;
   And first she spit fire and then she spit smoke,
   Lord, she gave a great lep and my shoulder near broke.

5 When at Balaklava we landed quite sound,
   Both cold wet and hungry we lay on the ground.
   Next morning for action the bugle did call,
   And we got a hot breakfast of powder and ball.

6 We fought at the Alma, likewise Inkermann,
   But the Russians they whaled us at the Redan.
   In scaling the walls there myself lost an eye,
   And a big Russian bullet ran off with my thigh.

7 They brought me the doctor who soon stopped the blood
   And he gave me an elegant leg made of wood.
   They gave me a medal and tenpence a day,
   Contented with Sheila, I'll live on half-pay.

The Magpie's Nest

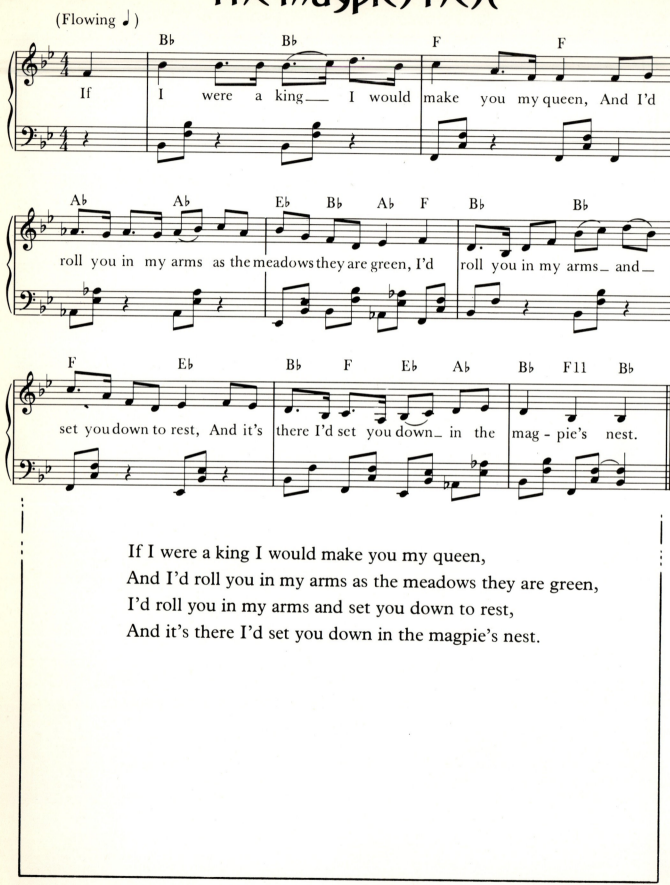

If I were a king I would make you my queen,
And I'd roll you in my arms as the meadows they are green,
I'd roll you in my arms and set you down to rest,
And it's there I'd set you down in the magpie's nest.

I Know Where I'm Going

1. I know where I'm going,
   And I know who's going with me,
   I know who I love
   But the dear knows who I'll marry.

2. I have stockings of silk,
   Shoes of fine green leather,
   And combs for my hair,
   And a ring for every finger.

3. Some say that he's black,
   But I say he's bonny,
   The fairest of them all,
   My handsome, winsome Johnny.

4. Feather beds are soft,
   And painted rooms are bonny,
   But I'd leave them all,
   To go with my love Johnny.

5. I know where I'm going,
   And I know who's going with me,
   I know who I love
   But the dear knows who I'll marry.

1 Down by the salley gardens
　my love and I did meet;
She passed the salley gardens
　with little snow-white feet.
She bid me take love easy,
　as the leaves grow on the tree;
But I, being young and foolish,
　with her would not agree.

2 In a field by the river
　my love and I did stand,
And on my leaning shoulder
　she laid her snow-white hand.
She bid me take life easy,
　as the grass grows on the weirs;
But I was young and foolish,
　and now am full of tears.

Index of titles and first lines

(The title is given only when it differs greatly from the first line of the song.)

A hungry fox one day did spy, 80
A little boy threw his ball so high, 64
A ring, a ring o' roses, 32
About four years ago I was digging the land, 122
Adieu to Old England, 102
American Stranger, The, 70
As I sat on a sunny bank, 109
As it fell out on a bright holiday, 110
Auld King Cole, 118

Baa, baa, black sheep, have you any wool? 20
Bitter Withy, The, 110
Blue-Tail Fly, The, 46
Bullfrog jumped in de middle of de spring, 50

Captain Kidd, 72
Cold blows the wind from east to west, 116

Doctor Faustus was a good man, 89
Down by the Salley gardens, 126

Farewell and adieu to you Spanish ladies, 88
First He made a sun, then He made a moon, 54
Fox and the Goose, The, 92
Fox and the Grapes, The, 80

Georgy Porgy pudding and pie, 22
Go tell Aunt Rhody, 56

Here we go round the mulberry bush, 36
Hey diddle diddle, the cat and the fiddle, 10
Holly and the Ivy, The, 108
How doth the little busy bee, 94
Hunt is Up, The, 76
Hush, little baby, don't say a word, 18

I had a little nut tree, 17
I know where I'm going, 125
If I was a blackbird I'd whistle and sing, 121
If I were a king I would make you my queen, 124
I'm a stranger in this country, 70

Jack and Jill went up the hill, 16
Jim crack corn, I don't care, 46

Kerry Recruit, The, 122

Ladybird, ladybird, 14
Little bird, little bird, go through my window, 62
Little Bo-peep has lost her sheep, 12
Little Boy Threw His Ball, A, 64
Little Nut Tree, The, 17
London Bridge is broken down, 30

Magpie's Nest, The, 124
Maid and the Miller, The, 77
Mermaid, The, 66
Mister Frog went a-courtin', he did ride, Uh-hum, 42
Mister Rabbit, Mister Rabbit, yo' ears mighty long, 60
Mocking Bird, The, 18
My Boy Willie, 98
My father he left me three acres of land, 96
My name was Robert Kidd, 72

O dear what can the matter be? 114
O once I could ride in my coach, 102
O rattling, roaring Willie, 120
O where have you been all the day, my boy Willie? 98
Oh! where are you going? To Scarborough Fair, 100
Old Grey Goose, The, 56
Old Ponto is dead and laid in his grave, 68
Old Woman Tossed, The, 78
One Friday morning we set sail, 66

Oranges and lemons, 28
Our auld King Cole was a jolly auld soul, 118

Rattling, Roaring Willie, 120
Ring o' Roses, A, 32

Sally go round the sun, 38
Scarborough Fair, 100
Shanghai chicken an' he grow so tall, 48
Short'nin' Bread, 44
Sing Ivy, 96
Sluggard, The, 84
Spanish Ladies, 88
Story of Creation, The, 54

The fox went out one moonlight night, 92
The holly and the ivy, 108
The hunt is up, the hunt is up, 76
The train is a-coming, oh yes! 52
There was a maid went to the mill, 77
There was a monkey climbed up a tree, 82
There was an old woman tossed up in a basket, 78
There were three jovial Welshmen, as I have heard them say, 86
Three blind mice, see how they run! 24
Three Jovial Welshmen, 86
Three little chillun, lyin' in bed 44
Three maidens a-milking did go, 104
'Tis the voice of the sluggard, I hear him complain, 84
Tom he was a piper's son, 90
Train is A-Coming, The, 52

Up in the Morning Early, 116

We're marching round the levee, 37
What's little babies made of, made of, 58

Yankee doodle came to town, 106
You turn for sugar, 34